BIG TRUTH little books®

Protecting the Flock: The Priority of Church Membership

Cliff McManis

D1616483

GBF Press
Sunnyvale, CA

Protecting the Flock: The Priority of Church Membership is volume 8 in the
BIG TRUTH little books® series.

General Editor
Cliff McManis

Series Editor
Derek Brown

Associate Editors
Breanna McManis
J. R. Cuevas
Jasmine Patton

Affectionately Dedicated to Tim Wong,
Faithful Elder and Shepherd of
GBF Membership Since 2006

CONTENTS

SERIES PREFACE

Our mission with the *BIG TRUTH little books*™ series is to provide edifying, accessible literature for Christian readers from all walks of life. We understand that it is often difficult to find time to read good books. But we also understand that reading is a valuable means of spiritual growth. The answer? Get some really big truth into some little books. Every book in this series is only 5″ x 8″ and around 120 pages. But each is full of Scripture, theological reflection, and pastoral insight. Our hope is that Christians young and old will benefit from these books as they grow in their knowledge of Christ through his Word.

Cliff McManis, General Editor
Derek Brown, Series Editor

~1~

THE MANDATE TO PROTECT THE FLOCK

"Be on guard for yourselves and for all the flock, among which the Holy Spirit has made you overseers, to shepherd the church of God which He purchased with His own blood" (Acts 20:28).

The Apostle Paul gave this urgent charge to the elders of the church of Ephesus on his third missionary journey. Paul planted the church in Ephesus and pastored it for more than two years (Acts 19). He poured his life into the people there, loved them dearly, and wanted them to be protected upon his departure. He entrusted their spiritual care into the hands of the local elders of that church, men Paul himself had raised up and trained. And here Paul makes one of the main responsibilities of an elder or a local pastor clear—to protect the flock; care for the sheep; help the local saints guard against false teachers, false teaching and compromised living.

How do local pastors guard or protect the flock? Many pastors are oblivious to this basic command. Other pastors struggle to adequately meet this heavenly demand. One helpful tool that practically facilitates obeying this pastoral charge is to have a formal church membership process. Church membership ensures that the shepherds know who their sheep are and the sheep know who their leaders and spiritual family are.

"To be, or not to be…a church member? That is the question." In this book, we are going to look at church membership and what the Bible has to say about it. I've served in five different churches over the years, including one church that did not have formal membership. The other four churches where I served had formal membership, which manifested itself in different ways. Each of these churches had different procedures concerning their membership process, and some churches took it more seriously than others.

Since 2006, when we started our church plant, Grace Bible Fellowship (GBF), I've met hundreds of believers who have come to visit or be a part of our fellowship. I have been exposed to a wide variety of church experiences that these people have had. And I've learned that there are many Christians who are not familiar with church membership; some even question whether it is in the Bible. Many churches simply don't have any kind of formal membership, including some very popular and large denominations. So for many believers, church membership seems like a new or foreign concept. I would posit, however, that church membership is actually biblical and not at all ambiguous or secondary. Membership in the local church is fundamental if you are a Christian.

Before discussing church membership it is vital to first define some key terms. The first one is "church." In the New Testament the word "church" is used in at least three different ways, referring to (1) the universal church, (2) the visible church, or (3) the local church.

The Universal Church

The universal Church refers to all those who have been saved by believing in the gospel of Jesus Christ since the days of the Apostles up until the coming of Christ. It includes believers who have died and gone to heaven, saints like Paul, Peter, and your believing great-grandpa, and it includes all believers alive today as well as those who will be saved in the future. It includes all Christians on earth and all Christians who now live in heaven. And it only includes those who are truly born again, not those who profess to be a part of the Church but are not regenerate. It is the universal Church that Jesus was referring to when He promised that He would build His Church and the gates of death would not prevail against it (Matt 16:18).

A sinner becomes a member of the universal church by believing the gospel (Rom 1:16)—that is, by admitting that they are a sinner who has been separated from God (Rom 3:23)—while acknowledging that only Jesus, the God-man, can save their soul through His death on the cross and His resurrection from the dead (1 Cor 15:1-3; Rom 10:9-10).

Christians don't do anything apart from believing the gospel to become a member of the universal Church. You don't join the universal Church; rather, God joins you to the universal Church the moment He saves you. Paul says that every Christian is supernaturally joined to the Body of Christ (the universal church) by the work of the Holy Spirit the moment the sinner believes (1 Cor 12:13). From that point on, every Christian is an eternal, spiritual member of the universal Church, which is the Body of Christ.

The Visible Church

The visible church refers to the church on earth, which is the Body of Christ living in the world—all true churches in every city and in every nation together. The visible church includes current believers, but it also includes those who are not truly born again but have managed to infiltrate the church. They are the unregenerate people who identify with the outward Christian church but are self-deceived and are not truly children of God.

Ultimately, only God knows the hearts of people, so only He knows for sure who is truly born again and who is not. So the visible church on earth has a mixture of true believers along with affiliate unregenerate professors of Christianity. And Jesus promised that He would sort out that confusion at the end of the age (Matt 7:21-23; 25:31-46). In the meantime, Jesus warned that weeds would be growing with the wheat undetected (Matt 13:26-30), and goats would mingle with the sheep. But both parties, the saints and the ain'ts, are co-mingled in the earthly, unglorified, visible church throughout the world.

The Local Church

The local church refers to local assemblies of Christians throughout the world. Each assembly is both an autonomous spiritual family in one location and a temporal manifestation—or satellite—of the universal Church. Each local church is like a separate outpost for the Kingdom of God. Each local church is to have its own elders and deacons, functioning as an independent entity while at the same time working in concert with all other true biblical churches.

Most of the uses of the word "church" in the New Testament (there are over 100) refer to the local church. For example, Paul wrote to the Corinthian believers saying, "Paul, called as an apostle of Jesus Christ by the will of God, and

Sosthenes our brother, to the church of God which is at Corinth" (1 Cor 1:1-2). For the purposes of this book, our discussion of church membership will be in relation to the local church as opposed to the universal or visible church.

Defining "Membership"

The other term that needs defining up front is "membership." This word is a stumbling block to some people because it conjures up troubling membership associations with man-made (and not biblical) organizations such as fitness centers, Costco, the local country club or the Moose Lodge. But that is not the kind of membership we are talking about.

Church membership is simply a formal commitment to a local church family of believers in Jesus Christ, and to its leaders. This is the church with which you affiliate and identify; this is the place where you are going to serve, the place where you are going to be fed, the place where you are held accountable, and the place where you invest your time, energy, talents, spiritual gifts and the blessings God has given you. There is a definitive leadership at this church that knows you by name and vice versa. You can identify with this church as your spiritual family, locally speaking. If someone asks you who your pastor is, hopefully you are able to give a specific name. This is what I mean by "church membership."

If you have an unshakable hang-up with the word "membership," then consider answering the following questions:

1. Which local church are you accountable to?

2. Who is your pastor and who are your elders?

3. What local church do you weekly worship with?

4. What local body of believers are you personally committed to?

5. What local church do you regularly and consistently support financially?

6. At what local church are you regularly and faithfully serving in a specific ministry to help build up that local church?

7. Do you know the pastors and elders personally at your local church and do they know you?

8. What local church is your spiritual family?

All these questions are best answered in the context of a specific church membership. Accountability, commitment, regularity, faithfulness, consistency, service, giving—all scary words for independent spirits living the life of rugged individualism we call the American way.

To the chagrin of a few, there is formality to local church membership. "Formality" is not a dirty word. There is a time to be formal and a time not to be formal. There is a time for everything under the sun (Eccl 3). Formality simply means having an objective and clearly delineated process where all interested parties have a common understanding and commitment to the cause. As such, I would posit that Scripture teaches that if you are a Christian, then you need to proactively pursue membership at a local church. I'm not arguing for everyone to immediately become a member of the church they are currently attending; I am arguing from Scripture that a genuinely born-again Christian needs to be a part of some local church at a formalized level.

In 2006, I wrote a book about basic disciplines of the Christian life, including church membership. Since then I've received feedback from many people over my chapter on church membership. Some folks who have come to our church over the past decade have given me some helpful feedback, which led to many fruitful conversations for me and for them. Some people have actually joined the church as a result of reading the membership chapter in tandem with discussing it with me.

But I've also had feedback that wasn't so positive, and I listened. I remember one instance when I received some feedback from folks who attended our church for a long time but never joined. They told me, "You have a lot of good things to say in your chapter about membership and joining, but there's one thing that I didn't agree with. I didn't like how you kept using the word 'formal,' as in *formal church membership*." We talked about that issue in depth, but I don't think they were persuaded. They argued that the formality of membership undermined "the priesthood of all believers" and the "freedom" they enjoyed with being an autonomous priest.

I received a similar comment from another brother who was honest with me and informed me that he had grown up in a church that never had membership. It was a foreign concept to him, so we talked about some Scriptures as well as the chapter I wrote. In the end, he was frank with me and said, "You know what it comes down to, Pastor Cliff? I just don't want to be accountable to anybody." His candid statement shocked me. But, in a way, it was a breath of fresh air. He was a Christian, and we were friends, but he never joined the church. Despite his honesty, I was incredibly concerned for his soul as he moved on to another church that had no membership and little personal accountability. I believe that put him in a vulnerable position.

In this book, we will look at a host of different Scriptures, as we make a case for biblical church membership. God wants every Christian to be committed, accountable, serving, faithful and protected in the context of a local church, and local church membership helps fulfill each of these goals. Let's look in the next chapter at a survey of Scriptures starting with the early church and Christ Himself to help us through this topic.

~2~

MEMBERSHIP IN THE EARLY CHURCH

"No one, after putting his hand to the plow and looking back, is fit for the kingdom of God" (Luke 9:62).

This sobering declaration is from the Lord Jesus Himself. He spoke these words to warn certain disciples who expressed apparent interest in following Him. He was telling them that if they were going to follow Him, then they needed to make a deliberate, formal commitment to join Him—with no looking back. Jesus established and maintained a high standard of accountability for His followers and that standard remains today in His Church.

The early church that Jesus' apostles established had a definitive local church membership pattern. In the early church, conversion to Christianity was immediately followed by joining the local assembly of believers. Such joining happened in a formal, accountable, long-term manner.

Today it is commonplace for Christians to go to church, but to never become formal members of any local body. Countless Christians all over the world never "join" the church, and many are even passionately averse to such a notion. Many others engage in "church-hopping." This is when Christians sporadically go to various churches "buffet style"—picking and choosing what they like from all the different options but falling short of ever committing to and identifying with one particular local body in any long-term manner. Many times the mindset is, "What will this church do for me—how will my needs and desires be fulfilled?"

Jesus Established Principles of Membership

The Church started with Jesus; He is the Head of the Church (Eph 5:23). He predicted that He would build His Church (see Matt 16:18). He first built His Church through the twelve apostles—the men who would serve as the ministerial and doctrinal foundation of the Church through their teaching ministry (Eph 2:20). Even in His own teaching, Jesus laid the groundwork for church membership in a parable in Luke 15. You may be familiar with this parable, but there's a good chance you've never thought about this parable in the context of church membership.

When my wife and I were in Israel a few years ago, our tour guide took us up on a hill that overlooked the valley in Bethlehem. We sat atop this hill for about thirty minutes, waiting for shepherds to come out and lead their sheep. Sure enough, there were a few shepherds who began making their way right through the valley by Bethlehem along the green grass.

These shepherds had a definitive number of sheep—just enough that they could actually count them. If we had asked one of those shepherds how many sheep he had, he probably would have been able to tell us the exact number. As a matter of fact, he likely would have known the identity and characteristics—maybe even the names—of many if not all of those sheep. This kind of attention to one's flock is typical of shepherds, both now and in Jesus' day. The shepherd's first priority is to know his sheep—how many he has, what they are like, their needs, their vulnerabilities, and their whereabouts.

The word "pastor" is synonymous with the word "shepherd," and a shepherd is someone who cares for sheep. In the Church, God calls elders or leaders of the church "shepherds" and the people "sheep" (see 1 Peter 5:1-4). The parallel is clear. Elders, bishops, overseers, pastors, or shepherds (these words are used interchangeably in the New Testament) of the local church are supposed to know their sheep. Pastors are to know who their sheep are, how many they have, what their needs are, and so on. That is in keeping with this parable that Jesus gave in Luke 15:

> What man among you, if he has a hundred sheep and has lost one of them, does not leave the ninety-nine in the open pasture and go after the one which is lost until he finds it? When he has found it, he lays it on his shoulders, rejoicing (vv. 4-6).

Such attentive, sacrificial care for one's sheep was commonplace 2,000 years ago in Israel, and it is commonplace in Israel today. Notice how this shepherd knows that he has exactly 100 sheep. If he has 100 sheep and loses one of them, a good shepherd who is in tune with his sheep and his responsibility over them knows when one has wandered off. He is not oblivious.

When Jesus asks, "Does [he] not leave the ninety-nine in the open pasture and go after the one which is lost until he finds it?" He is asking a rhetorical question. The implied answer is, "Yes, when a sheep goes missing, the faithful shepherd will immediately set out to find him." I love this parable because it is a beautiful picture of how a pastor is called to care for his people. A good pastor knows his congregation; he knows every person, and certainly every member (cf. Prov 27:23). He knows his members; he knows their names; and he keeps careful track of them.

This parable lays the foundation for what a church is to be like and how church leaders are supposed to care for their people. They are supposed to know their sheep—this fact is presupposed by Jesus.

One of the New Testament metaphors describing the church is "flock" (Acts 20:28), which means the people are depicted as the "sheep" (John 21:16) and the leaders are portrayed as "shepherds" or "pastors." Jesus was the Master Shepherd (1 Pet 5:4). As such, He's the ultimate authority when it comes to discussing the business of the Church.

Jesus said in John 10 that the Good Shepherd "calls his own sheep by name" (v. 3). Notice, they are called his "own"—the sheep belong somewhere, and there is a definite affiliation that is personal and intimate. Because they are members, this allows the pastor to "know them by name." If you don't join a church and become a full-fledged, accountable member, then how is the local church leadership supposed to know you by name and thus protect, provide, nurture, teach and lead you as one of Christ's sheep? It's ultimately impossible.

Membership Principles in the First Church of Jerusalem

The next thing to consider is that church membership is the biblical model. That is clear from the book of Acts, which chronicles the birth and growth of the first church in Jerusalem. The first church began in Jerusalem on the Day of Pentecost (Acts 2:1) when the Holy Spirit came down from heaven and took up residence in the first believers.

This church began with "a gathering of about

one hundred and twenty persons" (Acts 1:15). The fact that the Bible gives a specific number of people is significant. It means that someone in charge was keeping a formal head count of who constituted the First Church of Jerusalem. There were clearly identifiable members. Names are even mentioned in Acts 1:13-14. It was not a willy-nilly loose association of unidentified people meandering in and out of mob life.

This formal pattern of tracking specific numbers of believers continues through Acts as the early church continued to grow. Luke, the author of Acts, gives repeated updates of how many people were members of the first church in Jerusalem. Someone was counting heads and writing this important information down in the church ledger.

For example, on the Day of Pentecost Peter preached a powerful evangelistic sermon to thousands of people out on the streets of Jerusalem. Many were convicted of the truth and believed in the gospel. Luke says "that day there were added about three thousand souls" (Acts 2:41). The word for "added" (*prostithemi*) here is a very specific compound Greek word meaning "placed into" and speaks of a deliberate, calculated act of adding a select number to a greater, existing whole. In other words, the early church was keeping a careful count of those who were being added as new members to the body.

It is important to note that people were "added" to the church formally after they believed and then got baptized. The process of baptism was a formal step in the process of joining the local church (Acts 2:38; 8:38; 9:18; 10:48; 16:15, 33; 18:8). The early church knew nothing of people getting saved who then ignored or delayed baptism. The act of baptism was the first step in formally identifying with the local church. Sadly, today there are countless Christians who get saved and either put off baptism or never get baptized by immersion at all, and thus they disregard the clearly established pattern of the early church.

People continued to formally join the church at Jerusalem after the Day of Pentecost, for in Acts 2:47 Luke says, "the Lord *was **adding*** to their number day by day those who were being saved." The head count continued as the church grew and grew. The church flourished even more and mushroomed to the point where "the number of the men came to be about five thousand"! (Acts 4:4). So the church went from 120 people to 3,000 then to 5,000 men, not counting women and children. Someone was keeping detailed tabs.

The word for "number" here in Acts 4:4 is the word *arithmos* from which we get "arithmetic"—the science of the computation of numbers. The early church was scientific in its calculation as to who was joining the church. There was no informal, loosey-goosey, superficial affiliation on the part of the first Christians when it came to joining a church. Christians didn't church hop from one congregation to the next, eschewing any formal commitment to membership based on personal convenience or the latest preference. Church membership was taken seriously and considered a privilege.

I have no problem telling Christians that they need to "join" a local church. Occasionally some will say, "The Bible doesn't say we have to 'join' the church." And then I will say, "Actually it does. Acts 5:13 says that very thing." Luke says in 5:13 that local unbelievers did not "join" (KJV; NIV) the church at Jerusalem. Luke meant that Christians did "join" the local church at Jerusalem—and in a formal way. The NASB uses the word "associate" instead of "join." The Greek word here for "join/associate" is *kollasthai*, from the verb *kollao*, which means to cleave to something like glue—a permanent attachment (cf. Acts 17:34).

This same word is used in 1 Corinthians 6:16 when describing a man and a woman being "joined together" through sexual intimacy. It is also used to describe the relationship between a believer and Christ when they are "joined together" at the point of salvation (1 Cor 6:17). So this word "joined" is the strongest word-picture possible to describe a formal, intimate, inextricable joining of two parties entering a mutual relationship of the highest commitment. This is what the first Christians did— they "joined" the local church in Jerusalem as formal, "baptized," identifiable members!

According to the Apostle Paul

Paul was an apostle and church planter. He started many churches from scratch and trained up leadership in those churches to lead them when he departed. A definite number of people composed these churches. When he wrote letters to these churches, it was common for him to designate the church membership with specificity (Philip 1:1). In all his letters he names specific people in each local church (Rom 16:1-24; 1 Cor 1:14; Eph 6:21; Philip 4:2; Col 4:7-18; 1 Thess 3:2; 1 Tim 1:20; 2 Tim 4:9-21).

He wasn't just addressing some obtuse, nameless mass of humanity generically clustered in disparate locations. He wrote with authority, always expecting full compliance on behalf of his listeners. He could do so because he was writing to specific people with names and faces who were definite members in the local churches he worked with. This would only have been possible if there was a formal membership kept in the local churches.

Paul instructed Timothy to keep a "widow's list" at the church in Ephesus (1 Tim 5:3, 9-11). This was a formal ledger of women's names in that specific congregation who qualified for special care in that church. To qualify for the widow's list Timothy had to know the women's names, ages, marital status, monetary needs, and they had to be women who put themselves under the purview of Timothy's leadership on a regular basis. If there was no formal church membership, no possible widow's list could have been maintained.

Keeping a formal ledger of church members would have been quite natural for Paul, who was an ex-Pharisee and a former high-ranking member of the Jewish Sanhedrin (Philip 3:5). The Jews in Paul's day had religious services and gatherings in a place called the synagogue. Jesus even attended and taught in the synagogue (Luke 4:14-15). The early church modeled some of their religious practices after the synagogue (Acts 13:13 ff.; 15:21). To be a part of a synagogue one had to be a formal member. There were qualifications for joining, and when you got kicked out or your formal membership was revoked, you were said to be "unsynagogued" (John 9:22). So formal membership in local places of religious practice was the norm in Paul's day. To expect the same standard in the local church assemblies would have been natural for the Apostle.

Formal membership in the local religious assembly also would have been normal for Paul in light of the Hebrew Scriptures, the Old Testament, of which he was a master. There was much formality in the Old Testament. God required formal recognition, accounting and membership of the people with respect to their religious affiliation in numerous ways.

Jews had specific membership in the community based on their tribe and family name. They had to maintain specific, detailed lists of their genealogy to validate their legitimacy of service as a priest or other areas of service. A foreigner had to go through a formal process of circumcision in order to "join" the Hebrew community (Gen 17:12-14). This formal process of identifying God's people in the assembly carried over into the New Testament Church. And even in eternity God will continue to keep a formal accounting of membership in heaven as evidenced by the Book of Life, a formal registry of names of people who belong to God (Rev 20:12), as well as a book of names referring to those people who do not belong to God.

Another example of formal membership in the ministry of Paul is in Romans 16. Paul concludes his epistle to the local Church of Rome by greeting almost thirty people by name:

I commend to you our sister Phoebe, who is a servant of the church which is at Cenchrea; that you receive her in the Lord in a manner worthy of the saints, and that you help her in whatever matter she may have need of you; for she herself has also been a helper of many, and of myself as well.

Greet Prisca and Aquila, my fellow workers in Christ Jesus, who for my life risked their own necks, to whom not only do I give thanks, but also all the churches of the Gentiles; also greet the church that is in their house. Greet Epaenetus, my beloved, who is the first convert to Christ from Asia. Greet Mary, who has worked hard for you. Greet Andronicus and Junias, my kinsmen and my fellow prisoners, who are outstanding among the apostles, who also were in Christ before me. Greet Ampliatus, my beloved in the Lord. Greet Urbanus, our fellow worker in Christ, and Stachys my beloved. Greet Apelles, the approved in Christ. Greet those who are of the household of Aristobulus. Greet Herodion, my kinsman. Greet those of the household of Narcissus, who are in the Lord. Greet

> Tryphaena and Tryphosa, workers in the Lord. Greet Persis the beloved, who has worked hard in the Lord. Greet Rufus, a choice man in the Lord, also his mother and mine. Greet Asyncritus, Phlegon, Hermes, Patrobas, Hermas and the brethren with them. Greet Philologus and Julia, Nereus and his sister, and Olympas, and all the saints who are with them….Timothy my fellow worker greets you, and so do Lucius and Jason and Sosipater, my kinsmen (Rom 16:1-15, 21)

This was a very specific congregation of people. Only membership can account for the specificity by which Paul and his secretary address the people in the Church of Rome. They had formal commitment, affiliation and accountability. They knew who was there; they knew who the leaders were; they knew what the needs were; they knew who the gifted people were, and they knew who was hosting the church fellowships in their homes by name. This was a shepherd who knew sheep, which can only happen through the flock's commitment and loyalty to a local church.

According to the Apostle John

Another clear example of formal affiliation with the local church is found in Revelation 2 and 3. In about 90 AD, decades after Paul wrote to the church in Rome, the apostle John wrote to specific local congregations that had been planted in Asia Minor. These congregations had identifiable leadership as well as an identifiable flock:

- To the messenger of the church in Ephesus (2:1)
- To the messenger of the church in Pergamum (2:12)
- And to the messenger of the church in Thyatira (2:18)
- To the messenger of the church in Sardis (3:1)
- And to the messenger of the church in Philadelphia (3:7)

Each of these cities had one local church that believers identified with and to which they were committed. Each of these seven churches had unique traits, strengths and weaknesses based on the composition of the specific individuals in these churches. In the days of the apostles, if you were a Christian, then you identified with a specific local church. Every believer had a spiritual family in the local assembly where they regularly met with the corporate body for worship, prayer, fellowship, celebrating the ordinances and employing their spiritual gifts in service to other believers. That is the pattern of the New Testament and the model we are to follow because it is the expectation of Jesus Christ.

Today, many believers engage in competing models of "doing church" that are nowhere near close to the biblical model and actually undermine it. Today there are countless Christians who do church "remotely" by listening to sermons at home on the TV, Internet or their MP3's. They don't have a vital connection with the Body of Christ at large; they don't serve other believers; they don't worship with other saints; they don't have accountability from local elders; they don't pray with other believers routinely; they don't celebrate the ordinances with the community of saints. In essence, they have invented their own religion—being spiritual by personally contrived preferences and dictates instead of in accordance with God's Word as established by Jesus and the early church. Such shortsighted, myopic Christians see local church membership as superfluous and unnecessary. As a result, they stunt their own spiritual growth as well as the growth of the local church.

~3~

A Theology of Membership

Even though the word "membership" is not in the New Testament, the concept of local church membership and the principles of membership are clearly taught in the New Testament. At my local church there are three verses (passages) that serve as the foundation for our theology of local church membership. In addition to those three, there are dozens more that complement the theology of membership, many of which we will examine. But first, let's look at the big three.

Hebrews 10:24-25—Commit to a Local Church

The first passage suggesting membership in a local church is Hebrews 10:24-25 which says the following:

> let us consider how to stimulate one another to love and good deeds, not forsaking our own assembling together, as is the habit of some, but encouraging one another.

The author of Hebrews wrote his epistle to believers in the early church, and he exhorted these Christians to keep meeting regularly for corporate worship and fellowship. He was issuing two commands or expectations in this passage, and they are inseparable. The first command is that Christians need to regularly encourage one another. The second command is that Christians need to stop ditching church. If believers routinely ditch church and are missing corporate fellowship on the Lord's Day, then they can't fulfill the first command of regularly encouraging their fellow Christians.

The main reason Christians need to go to church regularly is to worship God corporately with God's people (Acts 2:46-47). Another main reason to go to church regularly, according to this passage in Hebrews, is so that you can minister to other believers by motivating them to love God and their fellow man and to encourage them to do "good deeds." This is by God's design. God made us social beings, and some basic Christian virtues and disciplines don't happen outside the context of gathering together as a body or community of believers. Certain elements of spiritual growth and maturity will not occur when a Christian remains in isolation or detached from the local church. Christians who forsake regularly gathering with the local church will undercut their own spiritual growth and become stunted while concurrently abandoning their divine obligation to stimulate others in the corporate assembly toward love and good deeds. For such transgressions, these non-committed believers are also subject to God's chastening and future loss of reward because of their self-centered lack of faithfulness toward the local body of believers (1 Cor 3:15; cf. Matt 25:26-29).

Countless professing Christians simply "attend" church like mere spectators waiting to be entertained at a sporting event, or like movie-goers who darken the theater doors occasionally and leave immediately as the credits begin rolling on the big screen. "Going to church" for such people is all about fulfilling the following narcissistic notions: "What will church do for me? Will I get what I want on Sunday morning? Was I satisfied with all the elements that came my way? Did the music entertain and soothe me? Did the preaching give me warm fuzzies and tickle my ears? Did people notice me and make me feel good? Was everything done to my liking?"

Such questions fly in the face of Hebrews 10:24-25. Going to church is primarily about giving God His due and about serving others, not being served. If everyone went to church with the sole purpose of being served, then no one would be served. If everyone went to church with the goal of serving others, then all would be served and edified. Having the priority of loving and serving others in corporate fellowship is basic biblical Christianity and Christlikeness. Jesus said that He came to earth not to be served, but to serve (Mark 10:45). Believers are called to follow Christ's example (John 13:14-15).

So principle number one from Hebrews 10:24-25 is clear: every Christian needs to be attending a local church regularly, weekly at least, for the purpose of serving other believers by encouraging them to love and perform godly deeds. If you are a church hopper, a nonchalant intermittent attendee, a hands-off laissez faire spectator, or an isolated Christian lone ranger, then you are disobeying a basic command of God.

Hebrews 13:17—Christians Must Submit to Local Church Leaders

The second verse that clearly assumes a commitment to a specific local church is Hebrews 13:17:

> Obey your leaders and submit to them, for they keep watch over your souls as those who will give an account. Let them do this with joy and not with grief, for this would be unprofitable for you.

A key question to answer here is "Who are the 'leaders' in this verse?" Is it talking about government or political leaders? No. Romans 13 talks about those kinds of leaders. Is it talking about various leaders throughout your life who had an impact on you at one time or another? No. Hebrews 13:7 talks about those kinds of leaders. Is it talking about church leaders at large that you listen to on CDs or watch on YouTube, that teach the Bible and that you admire but with whom you have no real relationship or accountability? No, not those leaders either.

The context makes it clear that the leaders it is referring to are those who currently "watch over your souls." "Watch over" is one Greek verb—*agrupnousin*—and is in the present tense in this verse. Therefore, it is talking about the spiritual leaders who are presently in your life, the ones today trying to help you grow spiritually—your present day local church leaders and pastors. Notice that the text refers to them as "your" leaders—church leaders with whom you have personally identified and with whom you have an understood reciprocal relationship. This is not possible unless you are regularly committed to and involved in a local church where you are known personally by the church leaders who shepherd that local congregation. These are "your" spiritual leaders at "your" local church that you are accountable to. They know you by name and you know them by name (cf. John 10:27). And since they are "your" leaders," that means that you are "their sheep." Local church pastors need to know who their sheep are, for it's that finite group of sheep that church leaders are to "watch over."

The verse goes on to say that local church leaders will have to "give an account" for how they watched over your soul. For me as a pastor, that is a sobering and even frightening prospect. All church leaders will have to give a personal account to Jesus the Judge for how well they pastored the souls He entrusted to their care. And the Bible says that spiritual leaders will face a stricter judgment (James 3:1) because of the authority delegated to them and the spiritual nature of the work—for eternal souls are at stake. In light of that truth, as a church leader I want to know who exactly my sheep are, by name, and which ones I have to give an account for. I don't want to be responsible for all Christians in Sunnyvale or all believers in Northern California— only the ones that God says are my sheep in the local church. In order to identify specifically who those sheep are, our church uses the mechanism of a formal church membership process to fulfill this biblical mandate.

Another priority to note in this verse is that there are two commands given to every believer. Every Christian is obligated to "obey" and "submit" to their church leaders. These are imperatives, not suggestions. To neglect these actions is to sin against God and His Word. To defy or avoid church leadership is to skirt and shirk responsibility and to disobey Christ. Following the leadership of local church leaders is a basic biblical discipline (1 Cor 16:16). Being under the authority of local pastors is foundational to spiritual growth (1 Tim 5:17). Respecting your church leaders is a rudimentary Christian obligation (1 Thess 5:12-13). Being accountable to your local church elders is healthy, a safeguard and what God expects (Acts 20:28). If you ditch church regularly or are hit-and-miss in attendance or are not committed regularly to the local fellowship of the Body of Christ, then you can't do any of the above. In addition, you will sabotage your own spiritual progress and sanctification.

Admittedly, the words "obey" and "submit" scare a lot of people. That's because we are all sinners by nature, and by nature we want to serve and please ourselves. Rebels don't want to submit.

Sinners don't want accountability nor do they want to be told what to do. So only changed, regenerate, Spirit-filled believers will want to obey and submit to other people and find joy in doing it. This requirement is by God's design, for it is His Church, and He has chosen to guide and direct His Church through fallen, finite, redeemed under-shepherds (leaders) who wield God's delegated authority to lead the Church in accordance with God's revealed will found in Scripture.

"Obey" means "to listen to" and "submit" means "to yield under." The two words together mean, "do what they say" or better, "listen to and follow their advice." God expects Christians to obey and submit to their church leaders. But it does not mean obeying and submitting in every area of life; it means obeying and submitting in the limited appropriate jurisdiction of church and spiritual life as delineated and outlined in the Bible. Those parameters of obedience are clearly revealed in Scripture. Church leaders need to give an account to God for how they led; church people are going to give an account for how well they obeyed and submitted to their church leaders. If you are not committed to a local church, then you can't fulfill this basic heavenly mandate of Hebrews 13:17.

On occasion, there are folks who attend our church over the course of months and sometimes years who never bother to pursue formal accountability through membership. All the while, they will enjoy the privileges we provide like the new, cushy pews; the state of the art air-conditioning system; the safe and fully staffed caring nursery; the excellent music; the well-prepared and biblical Sunday school lessons of our faithful teachers; the yummy four-course home-cooked lunches available after church at the fellowship meal; participation in communion and baptism; and listening to my 50-minute sermons, the by-product of twenty hours or more of arduous study each week. And these unaccountable, free-going non-members get all these nice services at no cost—absolutely free! What a deal.

Inevitably, at some point I will ask such regular-attenders in private, "When you are out and about and people ask you, 'Who's your pastor?' What do you tell them?" They will typically respond, "Well, I say 'Pastor Cliff ' —you are my pastor."

Then I tell them, "Wow! I did not know that. I'm glad I asked. That's actually kind of scary." They usually look at me with a curious, confused or surprised look regarding my response. Then I explain to them Hebrews 13:17. "This verse says if I am your pastor then I have to 'give an account' to Jesus for caring for your soul—and all along, until now, I did not realize I was your pastor...because you never told me this was your church or that you wanted to be committed to our body of believers. You have never taken any initiative at being involved, regular, accountable, consistent or shown any proactive signs of being willing to obey and submit to the elders here at our church. You expect me to watch over your soul but you don't expect yourself to obey and submit. If you are going to tell people I am your pastor then maybe you should formally pursue membership here so our elders will know about your intentions."

Most folks get the message very clearly during this conversation. As a result, many folks have felt convicted and stepped up and joined the church and also gotten involved in the local Body in obedience to Scripture. On rare occasions this conversation has scared a few folks away, because after all, accountability can be a scary thing. From all the preceding, it is clear that Hebrews 13:17 cannot be realized without a deliberate commitment to the local church—at Grace Bible Fellowship, we call that "formal membership."

1 Peter 5:1-4—Church Leaders Need to Care for Their Sheep

The third foundational passage establishing the precedent for local church membership is 1 Peter 5:1-4:

> Therefore, I exhort the elders among you, as your fellow elder and witness of the sufferings of Christ, and a partaker also of the glory that is to be revealed, shepherd the flock of God among you, exercising oversight not under compulsion, but voluntarily, according to the will of God; and not for sordid gain, but with eagerness; nor yet as lording it over those allotted to your charge, but proving to be examples to the flock. And when the Chief Shepherd appears, you will receive the unfading crown of glory.

The last verse we looked at, Hebrews 13:17, was a command for the sheep. This passage is a command for the shepherds. When both commands are obeyed at the same time there is supernatural, reciprocal harmony among the saints and the elders, and simultaneous blessings poured out by God.

The main command in this passage is at the beginning of verse two—the verb "shepherd." The main responsibility of church leaders, or elders, is to shepherd the people. Shepherding entails feeding

and leading, or guiding and providing. The New
Testament uses several verbs describing the priority
tasks of the shepherd:

1. the ministry of the Word (preaching, teaching,
and counseling with Scripture) (Acts 6:4);

2. prayer (Acts 6:4);

3. leading and oversight (1 Tim 3:1, 5);

4. protecting (Acts 20:28);

5. admonishing (1 Thess 5:12); and

6. arbitrating conflict (Acts 15:6)

All these actions together entail biblical shepherding
or pastoring in the local church.

The job description of the local church pastor is
clear. These six elements of shepherding are
ongoing, time-consuming, and highly personal;
several of them require personal interaction. At our
church of 250 people, our six elders are stretched
thin and maxed out trying to fulfill all of these

duties. We take these responsibilities seriously and literally. Therefore it is a priority for us to determine who we are obligated to shepherd. We ask, "Who are the sheep of our local church? Which specific people must we care for?" Our resources are limited, so we need to identify exactly who is in our local spiritual fold. Our six elders can't sufficiently shepherd an indefinite number of people. So how do we identify those for whom we are responsible?

Peter answers that question specifically in the passage. He says leaders need to shepherd the sheep "among you" (v. 1) and the ones specifically "allotted to your charge" (v. 2). Together these two phrases clearly define an objective and finite group of people we are to shepherd. The ones "among you" limit our responsibilities to the local church; and those "allotted to our charge" literally means "the specific ones God has entrusted to you." And the way we vet and identify who these sheep are is through the mechanism of our membership process.

So at our church, our elders are committed to specifically shepherding our members—the believers in our local assembly who have entered into a mutual relationship of commitment with us as defined by key biblical mandates in Scripture—passages like Hebrews 10:24, Hebrews 13:17 and 1 Peter 5:1-4. At our church there is no ambiguity as to who our leaders are, who our formal members are, who the regular attenders are, and who the ongoing visitors are. And this membership process has served the saints and the elders of our church very well the past decade. Churches that have neither membership nor a membership process will be hard-pressed to ensure their people fulfill Hebrews 10:24; they will have no justification for expecting their people to obey and submit to the local church leadership with any consistency; and they will be mired in an endless guessing game of trying to figure out who they are responsible for with respect to their shepherding duties.

~4~

THE BENEFITS OF CHURCH MEMBERSHIP

There are many benefits to having a local church membership. I have pastored in various roles in several different churches. They were all unique, and they were all true churches. Like I said, some didn't have membership, and a couple had membership in name or in their bylaws but did not have it functionally. A couple had a clearly defined membership process. The churches that had a clear, biblical, functional membership operated more smoothly and orderly than the churches who did not have membership. Establishing a biblical model of membership is to the benefit of church leaders and the saints in the local congregation.

The benefits resulting from having a practical, balanced, functioning, current, biblical local church membership process are many and fall into two broad categories: (1) benefits for the shepherds and (2) benefits for the sheep. We'll highlight some of those here. These examples are ones we have personally enjoyed at Grace Bible Fellowship for more than a decade. It also needs to be noted that there are other prerequisites to enjoy the following benefits, one of which is having a team of biblically qualified elders and deacons who are leading the charge in your local church. They need to be qualified in light of 1 Timothy 3:1-13, Titus 1:5-9, and 1 Peter 5:1-4. Church membership alone is not a panacea for all church ills. Obedience to other biblical mandates needs to happen concomitantly.

Managing the Church is Easier

The first benefit of having church membership is that it makes managing the church easier for the elders. God expects elders to manage the church well (1 Tim 3:4-5). God wants His church to function decently and in order, not chaotically or flippantly (1 Cor 14:4). Effective management happens when the manager can account for all the variables while minimizing the unexpected. Having a definitive membership allows the church leaders to know exactly who their sheep are and what the limitations of their jurisdiction are. Church membership ensures a finite, closed system of operations in the community. You can't effectively manage people if you don't know if they are committed to your local assembly.

Stewardship of Time and Resources

The second benefit of church membership complements the first—it allows pastors to be good stewards of their limited time and resources. If we have six elders at our church and 200 members and 100 non-members who are regular attenders, how are the elders supposed to allocate their time? At our church we prioritize our members when it comes to practical shepherding.

God told the elders to shepherd the flock of God "in their midst," overseeing the specific sheep "allotted" to their care (1 Pet 5). We consider our members as the ones "allotted" to our care, so it is our members who get our time and attention first. Our members formally belong to our spiritual family and they are the ones for whom we have to give account.

Church Discipline is More Effective

Third, local church membership facilitates the church discipline process. Church discipline is a basic ministry of the church. Jesus said it was essential. Many churches are ignorant of it, and I even know churches that avoid it deliberately out of fear that people might be scared off (cf. Acts 5:11). Here's the mandate of church discipline as Jesus gave it:

> If your brother sins, go and show him his fault in private; if he listens to you, you have won your brother. But if he does not listen to you, take one or two more with

you, so that BY THE MOUTH OF TWO OR THREE WITNESSES EVERY FACT MAY BE CONFIRMED. If he refuses to listen to them, tell it to the church; and if he refuses to listen even to the church, let him be to you as a Gentile and a tax collector. Truly I say to you, whatever you bind on earth shall have been bound in heaven; and whatever you loose on earth shall have been loosed in heaven (Matt 18:15-18).

The Church belongs to Jesus and He knows everything about it. He knows it will always be occupied by sinful people. When you get a bunch of sinners together, you are going to have problems, so Jesus laid down the process of dealing with sin and sinners in the church. It's a beautiful, concise, succinct, clear set of instructions for the church and its leaders. This process is supernatural, and it works.

The process has four clear steps that Jesus outlined in verses 15-18. In verse 17, after confronting a sinner with two or three people, if the sinner hardens his heart and doesn't repent after the second confrontation with these multiple witnesses, you are to escalate the confrontation. Keep in mind that this is a professing Christian. If he refuses to listen to the two or three that are confronting him, then they are to tell it the church. This has direct reference to the corporate local church. You go from two or three people confronting someone to now 200 people confronting someone, or if you're at a mega church like the church in Jerusalem, 3,000 people confronting someone. That's intimidating, but that's what Jesus has instructed us to do. You tell it to the church.

I believe Jesus' statement here has reference to the local church in which these people were affiliated. The local church is your spiritual family. Just as you have to confront sin in your own home among your siblings, spouse, parents, or your children and seek forgiveness and restoration and move on in the grace of God, so also should we have such a process in the local church family. If you're dealing with an unrepentant, hardened, professing Christian at this stage, you tell it *to the church*. That is what we do at the church at which I am presently a pastor.

Once a confrontation has come to the third step in the process, we gather all our members and we conduct a meeting in which we announce that this particular person has defied initial confrontation and has hardened his heart, and in obedience to Jesus we are now informing the congregation so that they might pray for this person and call the sinning member to repentance.

If the sinning member refuses to listen even to the corporate body of the local church and becomes even more hardened, then "let him be to you as a Gentile and a tax collector." In other words, this person is not acting like a believer, and at this stage the church is to consider the unrepentant member an unbeliever. The members are to pray for the recalcitrant member and minister to him accordingly, calling him to repentance and reminding him of the gospel. The point is this: you cannot perform church discipline like Jesus required if you don't have church membership.

The idea of not keeping formal church logs but instead simply informally welcoming all Christians into different areas of ministry sounds nice in theory, but it is neither practical nor biblical. And, unfortunately, one of the areas where this practice is most unwieldy is when a church is having a discipline issue. If you do not have membership in your church and there is someone who is divisive, cantankerous, and full of pride, and who is creating all kinds of problems through gossip and division, they need to be either shut down or held accountable. If someone in the church confronts the problem person and they don't give in, and they don't yield after two or three people confront them, you cannot bring this issue before the church because this person is not a member. You are left with no resources for accountability or consequences. A sinning non-member can flee anytime without consequence.

Many times, that person will simply leave the church with no accountability. As a result, an unrepentant, hardened, compromised professing Christian can easily leave one church and start over at another, and this new church will not have any way of knowing about any sinful patterns and behaviors because of a lack of church membership at this person's former church. If you have a membership process in your local church and there are other churches around you who also have a likeminded and biblical church discipline process, you can work jointly with local churches when it comes to church discipline. I have seen this work beautifully many times, just as Jesus said it would.

Membership enables the ministry of church discipline.

Dealing with Criticism

Fourth, church membership helps pastors deal with ongoing criticism in the ministry. There are some Christians who think their spiritual gift is nit-picking. Drive-by naysayers routinely church hop and take verbal cheap shots and pot shots at local church leaders as they are just passing through as the self-appointed neighborhood spiritual inspectors.

We have had our share of such rogue ecclesiastical quality control gadflies. They visit a time or two and then are in your face with suggestions such as, "Your announcements are too long." "Your songs are too contemporary." "You have too many hymns." "You need more topical sermons." "You need to start an evangelism ministry." "You should make all the children stay in the worship service." "You should make all the kids go to children's church."

"You should make people sit in different places each week." "You should start a soup kitchen." "You should have communion every week." "You should preach in a suit." "Why do you wear a tie?" "You shouldn't tell unbelievers to repent in order to be saved!"

Sadly these are not fictitious examples. When the people who give these edicts are visitors that our elders don't know from Adam, we have no obligation to cave to their demands on a whim. When our members give feedback, input and suggestions, that is a different story. We value the well thought out, prayerful, tactful input from our members since they are part of our spiritual family. Church membership is a beautiful thing.

Membership Facilitates Communication

A fifth benefit of membership we have seen is in the area of communication. A common weakness among churches is that the people don't know what is going on from week to week or month to month. It's not uncommon to hear church people say, "We don't know what the leaders are doing, how they make decisions or why they made the decisions they made." I have experienced that myself many times in churches.

I once worked on staff as an associate pastor at a Baptist church that did not have elders, but instead had a "senior pastor" and a board of deacons. The senior pastor was like the Pope; the board of deacons was like the college of Cardinals who wielded the power, and then there were the pastors on staff, like me, who served at the mercy of the Pope and the Cardinals. The deacons had a monthly board meeting with the senior pastor where all the planning and decisions were made for the church. Minutes were taken. But the pastors on staff were not allowed to attend the monthly meetings, nor were any of the members. We were not allowed to read the minutes of the meeting either. Decisions were delivered as edicts to be obeyed and we were to follow the oligarchy in blind faith. Decisions were routinely made in a corner with no explanation or context given to the people. This created great suspicion and a lack of trust. Clear, thorough communication to all the members was not a priority. Full disclosure to all the saints in the local church was not valued as a virtue. Dysfunction was the result.

At our current church, we believe open communication is a pre-requisite to church health. We believe the church is Christ's church, not "the leaders' church," and every member needs to be fully informed. All members are allowed to attend the monthly elder meetings. Every month the elders give the meeting minutes to our members so they can be current. All the members are issued a detailed report of the church budget on a monthly basis so they can see how much money comes in and how the money is being spent. When we select elders and deacons, our members are a part of the process and have a say about the prospective candidates. The leadership welcomes questions and the input from our members. God imparts wisdom through all of His people, not just the church leaders. As such, we value the perspective of our members.

Membership Provides Safety

A sixth benefit of formal membership is the safety it provides. I got this from one of the people who joined our church. I asked why she wanted to join the church. She said becoming a member will give her security—"it makes me feel safe." She went on to say that by being a member she knows the elders will watch out for her and care for her. She also knew that the membership process was a form of vetting that would help keep false teachers, predators and wolves from slipping into the local congregation. She also took comfort in knowing that, at our church, non-members could not serve in leadership positions. Only formally vetted members can serve as leaders in the nursery, as Sunday school teachers or as leaders with our youth. This gave her great peace of mind.

Membership Provides Motivation

A seventh benefit of membership is the motivation it provides for our members in several ways. Recently I asked one of our saints why they were joining our church. Her response was, "I need the accountability. I want to be challenged. I don't want to just come 'attend church' and then leave. I need the motivation that membership can provide." Another person who recently joined told me he wanted to become a member of the church because, "I don't trust myself! I am a sinner who needs regular accountability. I want the church to invoke the church discipline process on me if I need it." It was surprising to hear someone be so honest, but it was incredibly refreshing and a good reminder to me of the great value and benefit of real church membership.

Membership Guards Against Favoritism

As a shepherd-elder I am called to love the sheep—and that means all the sheep, and everyone who is a member at our church (John 21:15-17). Jesus loves all of His sheep the same. Local pastors need to do likewise (Philip 2:2). There is no room for pastors to show partiality toward certain people in the church. Sadly this is all too frequent. It is not uncommon for pastors to gravitate toward people in the church who will provide certain favorable results for the pastor or the church organization in general. I have seen first-hand "senior pastors" coddle congregants who happened to be big financial donors to the cause, or put certain people in positions of power in the church because they were influential businessmen, or golfing buddies with the pastor. At our church, our elders are committed to loving and serving every one of our members without partiality because we believe every one of them is a precious sheep who belongs to Christ's fold, and we are stewards of caring for them spiritually. Having a formal membership facilitates this shepherding perspective and guards against prejudicial treatment.

~5~

Why Christians Don't Join a Local Church

We have considered significant reasons Christians should become formal members in a local church and we have considered the many benefits of church membership. Now, let's take a brief look at why countless Christians all over the world don't become members despite the Bible's clear teaching.

Ignorance

One common reason Christians don't join the church is because of ignorance. Some believers just don't understand what the Bible actually teaches about membership. This happens because the truth is often shrouded by formal and informal man-made religious traditions, conventions and human opinion. There are actually churches out there that categorically condemn any kind of formal commitment and accountability to the local church, calling it authoritarian, cultic, oppressive, controlling and countless other baseless labels. They dogmatically assert, "The word 'membership' is not in the Bible." That is true, but it's a shallow argument because the principles of membership are clearly taught and mandated in the Bible. The word "Trinity" is not in the Bible but we know that God is one essence with three Persons. The fundamental truths about the nature of God are clearly taught in the Bible.

The word "Jesus" is not in the Old Testament, so are we to assume Jesus did not exist in the Old Testament era? Of course not. Jesus is all over the Old Testament. Paul recognized Jesus as YHWH of the Old Testament when he penned the book of Romans. John the Apostle called

Jesus God, who was the creator from the beginning of time (John 1:1-14), which is a clear allusion to the book of Genesis. The author of Hebrews declared that Jesus was the same yesterday, today and forever—meaning that Jesus is eternal and existed during the entire duration of the Old Testament era.

The human tendency through the ages when it comes to religion is to deviate from God's standard and what He actually says in His Word, and then supplant God's truth on any given issue with man-made teachings, regulations and customs. The teaching on church membership has not escaped this perennial vice. If this has been true with you then you can be comforted by Jesus' words when He said, "know the truth and the truth will make you free" (John 8:32). Doing things God's way—the way of truth—is always liberating and attendant with His blessings in your life. The basic principles of membership in a local church are taught in the Bible.

Church Background

A second reason people don't join the church may be due to their religious background. There are plenty of churches and denominations out there that formally teach that church membership is not taught in the Bible. I have met many Christians of this persuasion. I have had some wonderful Christian people attend and affiliate with our church who were saved or served for years at such churches that taught there is no such thing as required membership.

They like to say, "God's Church is everywhere, all over the world—He knows who His sheep are. He doesn't need a membership list." That sounds quite spiritual, but it simply is naive and not true, as we have already seen what the Bible says on this issue. But often times it is very difficult for people to shake the habits and predispositions they were raised with. It then becomes a matter of trying to re-inform or reprogram their conscience with biblical truth so they can overcome the roadblocks and hurdles of past thinking patterns.

Bad Previous Experiences

A third reason Christians don't join a local church is because they may have had bad previous experiences. Maybe they were at a church that misused the membership process to manipulate the people. Or maybe they were members at a church where they got burned by the pastor or the church leadership. That happens all too commonly, and that is wrong and it grieves Christ. There are actually a lot of bad and dysfunctional churches out there. Such pastors and leadership will have to give an account to God for their misuse of power (James 3:1). But someone else's sinful behavior does not negate what God commands and expects in other contexts. God still expects Christians to be committed, accountable, faithful, involved regular attenders of the local church despite any previous malfeasance on the part of another church.

A Lack of Commitment

A fourth reason people don't join the church is because they simply do not want to commit. That's how many people are these days—they don't seem to want to commit to anything, be it the church, marriage, relationships, appointments, a job, whatever. They want to reserve the right to do their own thing at any time on a whim.

It's not uncommon for many Christians to have hit-and-miss church attendance for the sole purpose of maintaining their busy leisure schedule, their highfalutin entertainment plans or their extensive travel calendar. "If I join the church," they fear, "then I can't do my own thing." Well...they are right. Being a part of Christ and His Church is not all about doing our own thing or doing what we want—it's all about doing His thing and what He wants (Matt 6:33).

Just Passing Through

A fifth reason people don't join the church pertains to sojourning. Occasionally we will have people attend our church who are in the area temporarily. They might be college students who will graduate and move on in a year or more. They can be military personnel stationed in our area for six months. They may be serving a short-term internship for their job for a quarter of the year. They are sometimes a newly married couple that anticipates moving across country in the next few months. So sometimes these folks think, "Well, we don't need to become members—membership is for long-term people." When we hear that reasoning we try to explain why it is not so. We believe God wants His people to be accountable to the local church wherever they are no matter how long they might be in a certain location. As a result we have had plenty of people join the church knowing they would be moving on soon. But it was to their benefit, for we purposely took care of them, prayed for them and helped them when it was time for the transition. They felt blessed as a result.

Fear of Accountability

A sixth reason Christians don't want to join the church is because they don't want to become accountable to anyone. As we noted earlier, sinners don't want accountability. They prefer to hide in the bushes (Gen 3:8). Some people don't want to be told what to do—they don't want to answer to anyone...at least not at church! This kind of independent spirit is pervasive in our culture, for after all—this is America—the place where rugged individualism is a virtue, where personal autonomy is prized, and where people are indoctrinated to have it *their* way; love yourself; do your own thing; look out for number one.

Becoming a church member means being willing to submit oneself and subject oneself to local church authority. But authority is despised in our culture. We are told not to trust authority. Popular bumper stickers and T-shirts enjoin us to "QUESTION AUTHORITY!" Submission, respect and honor for authority are despised, not esteemed. But God's Word is clear on this issue: "whoever resists authority has opposed the ordinance of God; and they who have opposed will receive condemnation upon themselves" (Rom 13:2).

Many people don't want to become accountable for how they use their time, treasures and talents. To do so is to become vulnerable or even exposed. This kind of living goes against the grain of secular society. It takes supernatural trust and faith to live that way—faith that only God can provide. But the Bible says, "without faith it is impossible to please Him" (Heb 11:6).

A few times, we have had someone begin the membership process at our church, and right in the middle of the process they get cold feet and decide to run for the hills, without warning or explanation to us. These people we never see or hear from again. In each case, it became apparent that those folks left due to the prospects of being held accountable, and for them that was a fearful scenario.

So if such a reluctant spirit characterizes you and has kept you from joining a local church, then pray and ask God to soften your heart with His Word and His Holy Spirit. Ask Him to give you the right attitude. If you pray with sincerity, you'll find that in time God will indeed answer that prayer and He will change you. He'll do it because it is His perfect will (1 John 5:14).

Too Burdensome

A seventh reason people don't join a church is that the process seems too intimidating at times. Becoming a member at some churches requires jumping through countless hoops, passing theological litmus tests, enduring twelve-week membership classes with inordinate homework assignments, and a host of other frightening and laborious requirements. With such rigorous prerequisites it's understandable why some people loathe the infamous membership process.

But it does not have to be that way. Sometimes, simply asking a few questions of the church leadership can alleviate unfounded fears. In most instances church leaders will graciously walk you through the process step by step, even accommodating special needs or requests you might have to help you through the process. If there is formality to the process, that's OK too. Being formal, thorough and systematic is not unspiritual. God wants the church to do all things with excellence and sober-mindedness (1 Cor 10:31).

Personal Differences

Another reason Christians might not formally join the church is because they may have a difference with the local church they are currently attending. This is a frequent occurrence. Some might resist formal membership if they disagree with the statement of faith, or maybe they don't agree with some item in the church constitution or philosophy of the church.

In such instances, a believer may need to ask why there are differences. One should consider if the disagreements are major doctrinal issues or secondary issues of preference. Tangential issues of preference should not preclude one from joining a Bible-teaching church. On the other hand, if the differences are over core doctrinal issues, then there is a problem. In any case, you may have to choose one of three options.

Option one is to realize that you are at the wrong church...if they are teaching something basic that is not biblical—heretical views on major doctrines, for instance. If a church denied Jesus' full deity, His virgin birth, the inerrancy of Scripture, the Trinity, salvation by grace through faith alone, and the like, then it would be best to find another church that taught the truth on basic issues. Don't compromise core biblical convictions. Also, don't try to reform any local church by thinking you can single-handedly overturn a local church's entire leadership, constitution, and history. That would just be plain divisive...and futile.

Option two is to consider the possibility that you might be wrong in what you believe about a particular key doctrine. This means you need to maintain a humble and teachable spirit. Ask what God might be trying to teach you in that situation. Maybe He is trying to teach you that you have bad theology in a particular area. That happens on occasion...to everyone. No one but the Trinity and the Bible has a corner on the truth.

Option three pertains to when someone has a secondary disagreement with the church, but not a major doctrinal dispute. There might be a difference regarding style, philosophy, methodology of ministry, or the personality of a pastor. Maybe a given church has good theology, but the music played and sung is not the style or brand of choice, or the lighting is too modern or archaic, or the attire is too stuffy or casual, etc. In such instances, if the church is an advocate to the basics of preaching, discipling, praying and serving in a godly manner then the mature thing to do would be to set aside your personal preferences and join the church in a committed manner.

The church might not even be doing a great job in any of these areas, but if there is at least a biblical conviction to pursue those things, then consider joining that church. Make that church a better and more biblical church by serving it with all your heart. Quit looking for the perfect church! It's not out there. When you serve in a local church, you are not there serving humans, you are there to serve God and Christ. "Whatever you do, do you work heartily, as for the Lord rather than for men, knowing that from the Lord you will receive the reward of the inheritance" (Col 3:23-24). That is the essence of being Christ-like. The Bible says we should "regard one another as more important than" ourselves (Phil

2:3). Be different and set a rare trend by asking yourself not what your church can do for you, but rather what can you do for your church?

The Fear of Man

A final common reason for not joining the church is the fear of man. We planted our church in 2006 and since that time we have had a surprising number of believers shy away from committing to membership due to the "fear of man." What is the "fear of man"? It is being more concerned with what people in your life think about an issue than caring about what God and the Bible say regarding that same issue (Prov 29:25). In other words, it is when you put human opinion over God's opinion. Or, it's when you succumb to the peer pressure of people in your life and you are afraid of how they will think of you or treat you if you make a decision that offends them or hurts their feelings...even if their desires conflict with what the Bible teaches.

I have seen independent college graduates

resist membership for the sole reason that they were afraid of what their mommy might think, whether that parent had a different religion or simply belonged to a different Christian denomination than our church. We have had people begin the membership process only to jump ship in the middle of the process due to fear of what their relatives might think about their new commitment to our local church. We have had parents come to our church who were blessed and wanted to join, but decided not to, only because their elementary or teenage children would miss their friends at the previous church. So the parents made an important spiritual decision based on the fear they had of their immature offspring.

There are legitimate reasons not to join a church, but the fear of man is not one of them. Jesus commanded His followers not to fear man, but only to fear God (Matt 10:28). He got more specific when He warned, He who loves father or mother more than Me is not worthy of Me; and he who loves son or daughter more than Me is not worthy of Me" (Matt 10:37).

CONCLUSION

We have labored above to show that the Bible teaches principles of church membership including its requirements and benefits. The local church is God's flock and Jesus is the Chief Shepherd. He has delegated the care of His flock to fallen and finite human undershepherds called pastors or elders. Local elders are tasked with caring for the specific believers in their midst, the ones allotted to their charge by God. This group of saints is a finite group of people made up of specific individuals. The elders need to know these people personally and by name. These local believers need individual attention. Having a membership process facilitates fulfilling the shepherding task.

The membership process in our local church is informed by biblical mandates and is deliberate and formal—but it's not overly burdensome. Following are the prerequisites for becoming a member and an overview of the process:

The Prerequisites for Membership

Prerequisites for GBF membership include the following:

1. the person is a born again Christian (John 3)

2. the person can clearly articulate the gospel (1 Cor 15:1-4)

3. the person has been baptized by immersion after salvation (Matt 28:18-20)

4. the person has read our Statement of Faith and believes the Bible is the ultimate authority (2 Tim 3:16-17)

5. the person is willing to submit to the leadership of the GBF elders (Heb 13:17)

6. the person has demonstrated a legitimate and peaceable departure from their previous local church (Rom 12)

7. the person is not currently under *legitimate* discipline from a previous church (Rom 12:18)

The Process of Membership at GBF

1. The first step for anyone interested in becoming a member is to first read and become familiar with our church documents which include our Statement of Faith, Philosophy of Ministry and Ministry Distinctives.

2. The second step is for the prospective member to meet with our pastor-teacher (lead pastor) whose job it is to give an overview of the process, explain the purpose of membership and to hear the prospective member articulate the gospel and give their personal testimony of how

they were saved. We only want born-again believers pursuing membership.

We require all our members to be baptized by immersion after salvation, which is the New Testament model. If the candidate has not been baptized by immersion, they can't become a member until they do. At this time the pastor will answer any questions the candidate may have regarding what they read in our church documents. During this time the pastor will also explain our theology of membership based on Hebrews 10:24 and 1 Peter 5 to make sure the candidate understands theses principles.

3. In the third step the member candidate attends two membership classes with our elder who oversees membership. We keep these classes fairly small, 2-6 people at a time, to preserve the personal and intimate touch. During these two classes

prospective members read through the Church By-Laws and remaining church documents. They learn about the history of our local church. They discuss the importance of spiritual gifts and other priority spiritual disciplines such as corporate worship, discipleship, giving and serving. Some practical written homework is given as well.

4. Step four is when the candidate meets with all the elders to share a brief version of their testimony, to articulate the gospel and to ask the elders any questions they may have. This meeting is usually not longer than thirty minutes. After this meeting the elders then vote regarding that candidate. With a unanimous vote, the prospect becomes a formal member. The vote is preserved in written form for church records. The elder over membership then notifies the candidate

that they have become a member. During this step, the new member is officially added to our church membership list, which we keep current.

5. The fifth and last step of membership is when the new member is introduced to the church body during announcements in a Sunday morning worship service. We want all our other members to see who our newest members are so they can be sure to formally welcome them to the family, pray for them and help them assimilate.

ABOUT THE AUTHOR

Rev. Cliff McManis has been in pastoral ministry since 1989. He graduated from The Master's College with a B.A. in Biblical Studies and earned an M.Div. from The Master's Seminary. He went on to earn his Th.M. and his Ph.D. in Ecclesiology from the Bible Seminary in Independence, Missouri. He is the author of *Christian Living Beyond Belief* and *Biblical Apologetics*, and editor and contributing author of *Rescued by Grace*. He has served in churches in southern California, Utah, Texas, and the San Francisco Bay Area, and has been the teaching pastor of Grace Bible Fellowship since its inception in 2006. He and his family currently reside in the San Francisco Bay Area.

Made in the USA
Las Vegas, NV
02 August 2022

52590679R00069